T0123718

Remember when...
A LOOK BACK AT SIMPLER TIMES

The Lapienski Sisters

WESTBOW
PRESS®
A DIVISION OF THOMAS NELSON
& ZONDERVAN

WestBow Press books may be ordered through booksellers or by contacting:

WestBow Press
A Division of Thomas Nelson & Zondervan
1663 Liberty Drive
Bloomington, IN 47403
www.westbowpress.com
844-714-3454

Because of the dynamic nature of the Internet, any web addresses or
links contained in this book may have changed since publication and
may no longer be valid. The views expressed in this work are solely those
of the author and do not necessarily reflect the views of the publisher,
and the publisher hereby disclaims any responsibility for them.

Any people depicted in stock imagery provided by Getty Images are models,
and such images are being used for illustrative purposes only.
Certain stock imagery © Getty Images.

Interior Image Credit: Kerri and Stacy Lapienski

ISBN: 978-1-6642-2232-8 (sc)
ISBN: 978-1-6642-2233-5 (e)

Library of Congress Control Number: 2021902071

Print information available on the last page.

WestBow Press rev. date: 8/3/2022

Introduction

For quite some time, I have noticed that today's technology has allowed younger generations to grow up in a completely different way. My sister and I discussed the different generational gaps, and how there must be a way to remind people of simpler times and traditions. As we started talking about our own childhood memories, and after speaking with our close friends and family, this book was born.

We found that the more friends and family we spoke to, the more we learned about those individuals and even more about our own childhood experiences. It made us become even closer to our family, and we discussed bringing back some of the traditions that we had put away. We also found that everyone loved sharing their stories and seemed happiest when they took a walk down memory lane.

It is our hope readers will find this book makes them feel the same way. We hope it starts a conversation to recall all those simpler times in life that made them happy. And who knows, perhaps it will encourage them to re-engage in those activities and traditions that may have been put aside.

Great memories bring comfort, hope, closeness, and are a constant reminder to never forget what really matters.

—The Lapienski sisters

Dedication

To our parents,

For raising us to believe that anything is possible
and family is first.

1. ♦ The kitchen was completely filled with freshly baked Christmas cookies from family recipes.

2. ♦ We played manhunt in the neighborhood, when the neighbors didn't mind kids using their yard.

3. ♦ We went to drive-in movies as a family, bringing our pillows and snacks.

4. ♦ We played "make believe" because there were only three channels on TV, and we had to be creative.

5. ♦ We spent a few weeks at our grandparents' house every summer.

6. ♦ We would get our mouths washed out with soap when we talked back to our parents or said a bad word.

7. ♦ We would go to the beach as a family and the standard "beach lunch" was peanut butter-and-jelly sandwiches with chips.

8. ◆ When kids feared getting in trouble with their parents.

9. ◆ You shared a room with a sibling and chatted all night about everything.

10. ◆ When we lost a tooth, and felt so lucky when we found a dollar from the Tooth Fairy under our pillow in the morning.

11. ♦ When we drank out of the hose in the summer.

12. ♦ Having birthday parties at home as a kid, with little loot bags, games and cake.

13. ♦ When you had chores to do around the house and there was no allowance.

14. ♦ When you got a group of people together and went door-to-door Christmas caroling.

15. ♦ Packing some belongings in a pillowcase and running away to the backyard.

16. ♦ Baking family Christmas cookies with our grandmother, mom, and siblings.

17. ♦ Visiting family members' gravesides to pay respects and leave flowers.

18. ♦ When a playroom at church was *not* an option, and we had to sit still and quiet on those hard pews, or else!

19. ♦ Eating dinner each night no later than five thirty with the family to discuss each person's day.

20. ♦ When people were kinder and more considerate.

21. ♦ When friends and family would just stop by the house when they saw the front door open.

22. ♦ How simple life used to be.

23. ♦ When we had to use *TV Guide* to see when the Christmas specials would be on. If we missed them, we would have to wait another year to see them.

24. ♦ When kids played kick the can, kickball, and wiffle ball in the street and created makeshift bases.

25. ♦ When swinging from a wooden tree swing was hours of entertainment.

26. ♦ Mom called you inside from playing once the streetlights came on.

27. ♦ I remember going to Ireland where my mom grew up, played in the ocean and rode donkeys.

28. ♦ You ran outside when you heard the music from the ice-cream truck coming.

29. ♦ You played red light, green light, one, two, three.

30. ◆ Kids caught lightning bugs in a jar during the summer and poked holes in the lid for air.

31. ◆ Sliding down the stairs on a piece of cardboard.

32. ◆ When you had dinner every Sunday at your grandparents' house.

33. ♦ When you drank freshly made wine an Italian neighbor made from his own grapes.

34. ♦ When Mom said, "Wait until your father gets home," and you were actually scared.

35. ♦ The rope swing into the lake.

36. ♦ I remember when I brought a stray dog into my bedroom, thinking I could hide it from my parents.

37. ♦ When you emptied the pantry and used your dad's calculator to play "supermarket".

38. ♦ I remember playing games like "washing machine" and "Marco Polo" all day in the pool with my cousins.

39. ♦ You perused the *Sears Christmas Wish Book* and made a ridiculous Christmas list.

40. ♦ Christmas trees were decorated with handmade ornaments.

41. ♦ I remember playing stickball, punch ball, slap ball, and poker in the streets of Astoria.

42. ♦ You went ice-skating on the rink in Rockefeller Center.

43. ♦ I remember when my parents would put us in the car in our pajamas at Christmastime with blankets and pillows to ride around looking at Christmas lights.

44. ♦ I remember my grandmother and I would sit in her sunporch and work on jigsaw puzzles together. We had the most relaxed and amazing conversations. I learned a lot about her and her life.

45. ◆ When you set up a lemonade stand at the foot of the driveway in the summer.

46. ◆ I remember crabbing off the Patchogue dock with my dad. I was delighted to find them with a flashlight and scoop them up.

47. ◆ Learning to drive on a stick shift at sixteen.

48. ♦ When you made snow angels in fresh snow.

49. ♦ When you could get a hamburger and a Coke for a dollar at our after-school hangout.

50. ♦ When we rode our bikes everywhere.

51. ♦ When swimming in the pool was *fun*.

52. ♦ I remember playing outside *all the time*! We didn't come in until the streetlights turned on!

53. ♦ *Schoolhouse Rock!* on Saturday-morning TV.

54. ♦ There was nothing like a good snowball fight with good friends.

55. ♦ Family dinners were not buffet style.

56. ♦ You sat at the "kiddie table" for holidays and got in trouble for being disruptive.

57. ♦ Riding the steeplechase horses at Coney Island.

58. ♦ I remember feeding the ducks with my grandma at the pond.

59. ♦ Putting on little "plays" for the family on the holidays.

60. ♦ I remember ice skating at the cove until we were numb!

61. ◆ When you played Frisbee in the
street.

62. ◆ The innocence of believing in
magical things like Santa Claus,
the Easter Bunny, and the tooth
fairy.

63. ♦ I remember the smells of Grandma's best comfort foods, made with love in her kitchen.

64. ♦ I remember catching grasshoppers with my friends.

65. ♦ When you rode your bicycle through a deep puddle after a rainstorm.

66. ♦ Swinging so high on the metal swing set in the backyard that the poles lifted out of the ground.

67. ♦ Running through the sprinkler in the front yard on a hot summer day.

68. ♦ Taking every available blanket and making a giant fort in the living room.

69. ♦ Playing hopscotch.

70. ♦ The Sunday afternoon family drive.

71. ♦ I remember drinking Shirley Temple's at the kids' table on the holidays at my grandparents' house.

72. ♦ You carved pumpkins at Halloween to make jack-o'-lanterns.

73. ♦ Playing dress-up with mom's high heels and costume jewelry.

74. ♦ The excitement and the wonder of Christmas morning at six years old.

75. ♦ When people went on scavenger hunts.

76. ♦ I remember waiting for the digital clock in my bedroom to read 7:00 a.m. so I could wake up my parents on Christmas morning!

77. ♦ Pretending to be asleep on Christmas Eve, hoping to catch a glimpse of Santa.

78. ♦ When Mom dressed us in
       identical outfits on the holidays.

79. ♦ Leaving out milk and cookies for Santa, and carrots and water for the reindeer.

80. ♦ I remember when my parents made me a robot Halloween costume using a box for the body and spray-painted dryer hoses for the arms.

81. ♦ I remember kneeling on the floor next to the bed to say my prayers at night. Dad was in the middle, and my sister was on the other side of him. We would say them aloud together.

82. ◆ I remember helping my grandmother set the table for Thanksgiving dinner a day early.

83. ◆ Going sleigh riding and laughing until your stomach hurt.

84. ◆ Laying in our dog's bed.

85. ♦ When Mom would check for monsters under the bed or in the closet.

86. ♦ The water balloon fights in the summer.

87. ♦ Giving your brother or sister a haircut and your Mom freaking out about it.

88. ♦ Playing punch buggy in the car on a road trip.

89. ♦ You went to the Christmas parade in town and personally handed the postman your letter to Santa.

90. ♦ We would "pasear"(drive around) and go to the beach where they had a dog track on the beach. We would go to Lummus park and back and watch the old people dance to big band music from the wall. On the way home we go to McDonald's to eat, then Churros, then go home.

91. ♦ I remember the little gifts my
dad would bring me every
weekend during the summer.
He worked in the city and only
came to our country house on
weekends. I really miss that.

92. ♦ I remember growing up, my
cousins were my best friends.

93. ♦ When school closed for a
snow day.

94. ♦ I couldn't wait to go to my aunt's
house over the weekend to be
with her and my cousins. She
taught me so much.

95. ◆ Spending Saturdays at the movies, watching different films for a nickel.

96. ◆ Saturday-night streetcar racing.

97. ◆ Roller-skating to disco music at the roller rink in the eighties.

98. ♦ The sock hops.

99. ♦ The Saturday-morning cartoon marathons.

100. ♦ Neighborhood kids coming over for fun.

101. ◆ Drive-in movies and stuffing as many people in the car as we could because the charge was per carload.

102. ◆ I remember night fishing at Mill Pond, sneaking through people's backyards to get to the best fishing spots!

103. ◆ Pretending to live in a snow village.

104. ♦ I remember hanging all the Christmas cards we received around the living room archway. There were *so* many. Now we hardly receive any cards.

105. ♦ I remember riding my little blue tricycle as fast as I could past the huge stone walls of the Kensico Dam with my grandmother.

106. ♦ When women wore Easter bonnets.

107. ♦ Dressing up for Easter.

108. ♦ I remember my grandmother
had two wingback chairs
in her living room and two
grandchildren. Every Easter,
she always hid giant chocolate
bunnies, almost as big as we
were, behind each chair.

109. ♦ When summer seemed to last forever.

110. ◆ How much fun it was to hang out in a tree house.

111. ◆ I remember an ornamental horn my mother always put out at Christmas. One Christmas Eve, we made a game out of trying to see who could make the horn blow a noise, which it never did, because it was an ornament. A lot of people got very light-headed!

112. ◆ When we were seven years old, and we went to bed at eight, but it was still light outside in the summer.

113. ♦ I remember making homemade greeting cards for my parents for birthdays, Valentine's Day, and Christmas.

114. ♦ When the Good Humor man wore a white uniform.

115. ♦ Eating the cream off the top
of the fresh milk with a spoon
when the milkman delivered it.

116. ♦ Paper dolls.

117. ♦ I remember going to the
town pool every day. We took
swimming lessons and had
a pageant at the end of the
summer.

118. ♦ When the family dog ate table scraps and shared a bed with its owners.

119. ♦ I remember my cousins and I trimming string beans with my grandmother that had just been picked from the garden.

120. ♦ Sneaking out of the house to meet friends after your parents thought you had gone to bed.

121. ♦ I remember simple birthday party games, like dropping clothespins into a milk bottle and trying to carry an egg on a spoon.

122. ♦ Sack races.

123. ♦ Placing a whoopee cushion under any cushion you could find.

Innocence

124. ♦ Toasting marshmallows in the toaster oven since we didn't have a fire pit.

125. ♦ Taking a nap in a hammock on a Sunday afternoon.

126. ♦ Rotary phones.

127. ♦ Phone booths.

128. ♦ I remember Grandma's traditional Christmas candy bowl with Russell Stover Satins and Chips in it.

129. ♦ When most families lived on the same block.

130. ♦ Skipping rocks on the lake.

131. ♦ When Mom had coffee cake set aside in case anyone came over to visit.

132. ◆ Playing marbles.

133. ◆ Making Christmas cookies with
     the neighborhood kids and
     having them decorate them.

134. ♦ Drinking about a gallon of water before going to bed on Christmas Eve so I could wake up early and be alone with my presents because I had so many siblings.

135. ♦ My parents used to take me for a pony ride every weekend, same place, same horse.

136. ♦ My family and I would go boating every Sunday.

137. ♦ Staying up until midnight so we could open one Christmas present.

138. ♦ Making Christmas art.

139. ♦ Having helpers to make Christmas cookies.

Always remember...

To be present with people at a restaurant or at a party, instead of worrying about posting pictures on Facebook.

FaceTime can never take the place of a face-to-face visit with the family.

Texting is not the same as calling someone and talking to them on the phone.

Bring back Sunday family dinner, even if it is just for one Sunday per month.

Celebrate the holidays together.

Realize how much time we spend looking at other people's lives on Facebook instead of living our own.

Be kind.

Hold the door open for the next person.

Be humble.

Have manners.

Offer assistance or call the police for a stranded motorist.

Remember loved ones who have passed at Christmas.

Calverton National Cemetery

Be a great witness to an accident—that person is someone's family member.

Play a board game.

Go talk to family members rather than texting them from another room.

Have meals around the table.

Support local businesses instead of purchasing online whenever possible.

Volunteer and give back to the community.

Laugh every day.

Never lose faith.

Always look for a higher power.

Don't miss important family events because of work. Work will always be there, but those moments will not.

Life goes by very quickly.

Keep your heart open.

Try to be a blessing to others.

Always appreciate parental advice. There will be a day when you will give anything to hear them speak again.

Have the kids help decorate Christmas cookies—it gives the activity so much more meaning.

Accept the china and belongings family members leave behind after they're gone.

Hug often.

Pray every day.

Donate extra money to someone who could use the help.

Forgive.

Remember to include God; he is there waiting.

Sunset

Printed in the United States
by Baker & Taylor Publisher Services

Printed in the United States
by Baker & Taylor Publisher Services